Thank you...

... *for purchasing this copy of our Times Tables Resource Book. We hope that you find our materials helpful as part of your programme of numeracy activities.*

Please note that photocopies can only be made for use by the purchasing institution. Supplying copies to other schools, institutions or individuals breaches the copyright licence. Thank you for your help in this.

This Times Tables Resource Book is part of our growing range of educational titles. Most of our books are individual workbooks but, due to popular demand, we are now introducing a greater number of photocopiable titles especially for teachers. You may like to look out for:

READING FOR LITERACY *for ages 5-7, 7-8, 8-9, 9-10, 10-11*

WRITING FOR LITERACY *for ages 5-7, 7-8, 8-9, 9-10, 10-11*

SPELLING FOR LITERACY *for ages 5-7, 7-8, 8-9, 9-10, 10-11*

NUMERACY TODAY *for ages 5-7, 7-9, 9-11*

HOMEWORK TODAY *for ages 5-7, 7-8, 8-9, 9-10, 10-11*

BEST HANDWRITING *for ages 4-7, 7-11*

WET PLAY TODAY *for ages 5-7, 7-9, 9-11*

To find details of our other publications, please visit our website: **www.acblack.com**

Teachers' Notes

For pupils to learn their tables effectively they need to repeat the full sentence for each element of each table. For example, repeat 'one times two is two', 'two twos are four', etc, rather than simply learning 'two', 'four', 'six', 'eight' etc.

We recommend practising each table from one to ten for just a few minutes every day for a week. Keep Sheet A displayed on the wall and show Sheet B on the OHP as you practise the table.

When using the worksheets it is not necessary nor desirable to cover the table displayed on the wall. Every time a child looks at even part of a table some learning takes place.

Ideally at the end of one week of daily practice, each child should be tested individually but within a small group. Using a stopwatch to time how quickly an individual can recite the table can create a semi-competitive atmosphere. This has to be administered with care and diplomacy to ensure that individuals are not put under embarrassing pressure, bearing in mind that there will be a small number of children who simply cannot seem to learn the tables however hard they practise. Many children though become very excited to find that they can recite a complete table, to ten times the number, in less than fifteen or even ten seconds.

Of course, when practising a new table, the previous one gets forgotten! But, when next visited, the first table will be much easier to recall and will eventually be known thoroughly.

Contents

Two Times Table

OHP Display A

1 x 2 = 2

2 x 2 = 4

3 x 2 = 6

4 x 2 = 8

5 x 2 = 10

6 x 2 = 12

7 x 2 = 14

8 x 2 = 16

9 x 2 = 18

10 x 2 = 20

11 x 2 = 22

12 x 2 = 24

Look:

0 x 2 = 0

Two Times Table

OHP Display B

One times two is two.	1 x 2 = 2
Two twos are four.	2 x 2 = 4
Three twos are six.	3 x 2 = 6
Four twos are eight.	4 x 2 = 8
Five twos are ten.	5 x 2 = 10
Six twos are twelve.	6 x 2 = 12
Seven twos are fourteen.	7 x 2 = 14
Eight twos are sixteen.	8 x 2 = 16
Nine twos are eighteen.	9 x 2 = 18
Ten twos are twenty.	10 x 2 = 20

Eleven twos are twenty-two.	11 x 2 = 22
Twelve twos are twenty-four.	12 x 2 = 24

Don’t forget this one:

Zero times two is zero.	0 x 2 = 0

Two Times Table

Worksheet Name: Date:

The more you practise...

...the better you get.

Fill in all the gaps.

1 x 2 = ☐
2 x 2 = ☐
3 x 2 = ☐
4 x 2 = ☐
5 x 2 = ☐
6 x 2 = ☐
7 x 2 = ☐
8 x 2 = ☐
9 x 2 = ☐
10 x 2 = ☐
11 x 2 = ☐
12 x 2 = ☐

Now write out the two times table up to ten as quickly as you can. Write one line at a time and say it as you write it.

____
____
____
____
____
____
____
____
____
____

Match the questions to the answers.

0 x 2 =	14
1 x 2 =	6
2 x 2 =	0
3 x 2 =	22
4 x 2 =	8
5 x 2 =	10
6 x 2 =	16
7 x 2 =	20
8 x 2 =	2
9 x 2 =	12
10 x 2 =	4
11 x 2 =	24
12 x 2 =	18

Use the two times table to help you.

20 ÷ 2 =	7
22 ÷ 2 =	9
14 ÷ 2 =	2
6 ÷ 2 =	10
2 ÷ 2 =	5
8 ÷ 2 =	11
18 ÷ 2 =	12
24 ÷ 2 =	6
4 ÷ 2 =	8
10 ÷ 2 =	3
16 ÷ 2 =	4
12 ÷ 2 =	1

Two Times Table

OHP Display

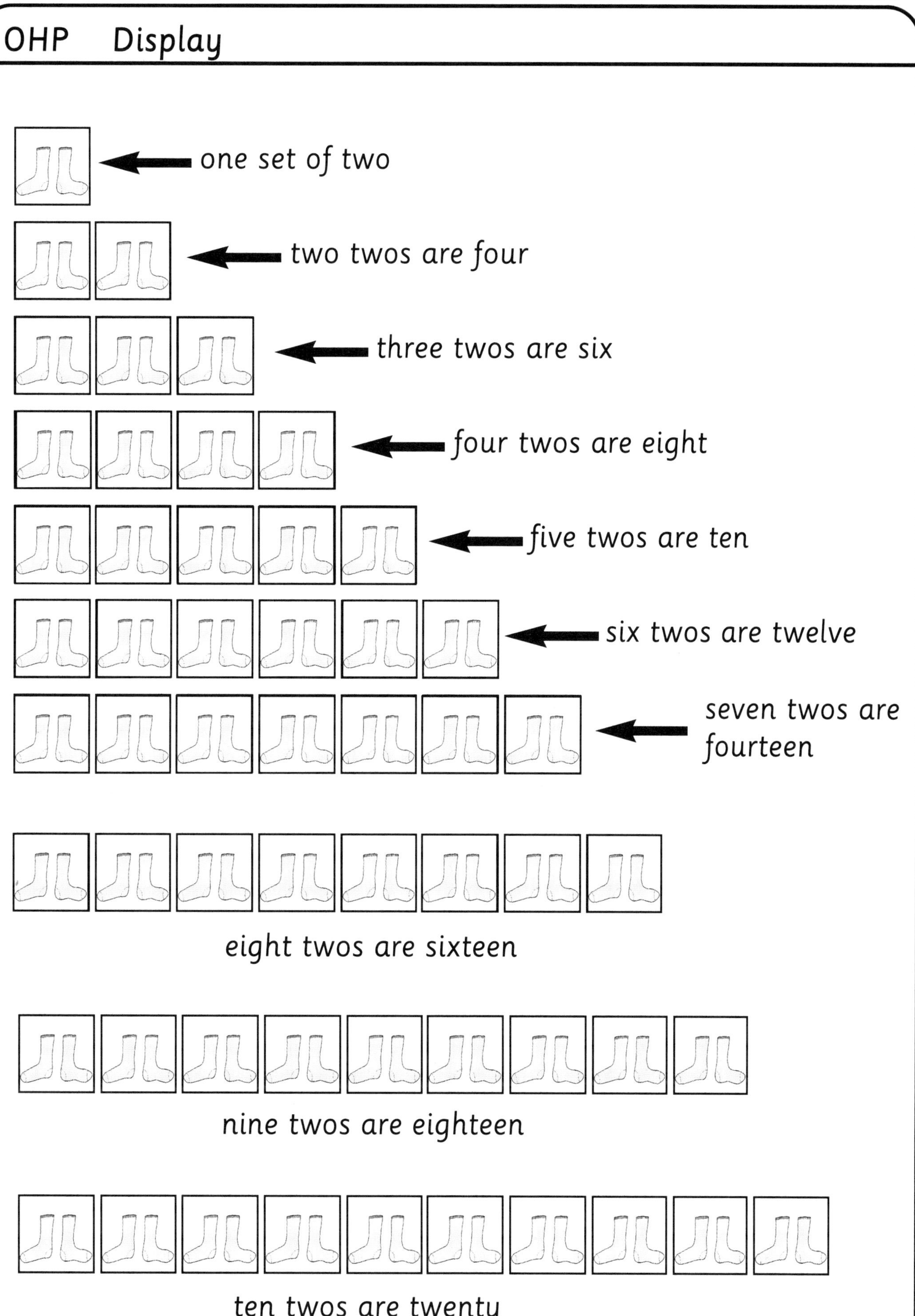

Two Times Table Game

START

2 4 6 8 10 12

14

28 26 24 22 20 18 16

30

32 34 36 38 40 42 44 46

48

You must land here to win.

50

52

66 64 62 60 58 56 54

68

This is as far as you can go.

70 72

Two Times Table

Game

A game for two players.

You need: two dice
two coloured counters.

The winner is the first person to land exactly on 50.

How to play:

* Place both counters on the start.
* Roll one dice each to see who starts first.
* Player 1 rolls a dice, then multiplies the score by two. Player 1 then moves forward the number of spaces given by this multiple.
* Player 2 now has a turn.
* Continue to take turns to play. (Make sure that you add your score to your previous position, then move to the square given. <u>Do not</u> just count on.)
* The winner is the first player to land <u>exactly</u> on 50.
* Any player who goes past 50 has to subtract, instead of adding, on his/her turn.
* Make the game more difficult by rolling two dice each turn instead of one.

Three Times Table

OHP Display A

1 x 3 = 3

2 x 3 = 6

3 x 3 = 9

4 x 3 = 12

5 x 3 = 15

6 x 3 = 18

7 x 3 = 21

8 x 3 = 24

9 x 3 = 27

10 x 3 = 30

11 x 3 = 33

12 x 3 = 36

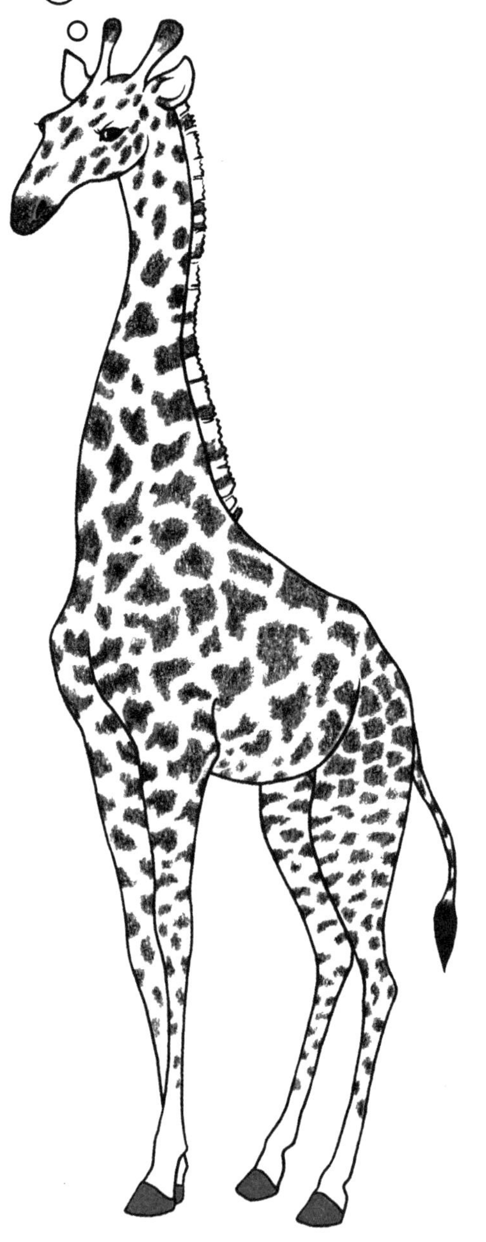

Look:

0 x 3 = 0

Three Times Table

OHP Display B

Keep saying the three times table.

One times three is three.	1 x 3 = 3
Two threes are six.	2 x 3 = 6
Three threes are nine.	3 x 3 = 9
Four threes are twelve.	4 x 3 = 12
Five threes are fifteen.	5 x 3 = 15
Six threes are eighteen.	6 x 3 = 18
Seven threes are twenty-one.	7 x 3 = 21
Eight threes are twenty-four.	8 x 3 = 24
Nine threes are twenty-seven.	9 x 3 = 27
Ten threes are thirty.	10 x 3 = 30

Some people like to learn eleven times three and twelve times three.

Eleven threes are thirty-three.	11 x 3 = 33
Twelve threes are thirty-six.	12 x 3 = 36

Don't forget this one:

Zero times three is zero.	0 x 3 = 0

Three Times Table

Worksheet Name: Date:

Fill in all the gaps.

1 x 3 =		
2 x ___ ___		
___ ___ ___ ___		
4 x 3 =	12	
___ ___ ___ ___		
___ ___ ___ ___		
___ ___ ___ ___		
8 x 3 =	24	
___ ___ ___ ___		
___ ___ ___ ___		
___ ___ ___ ___		
12 x 3 =	36	

Match the questions to the answers.

0 x 3 =	24
1 x 3 =	6
2 x 3 =	0
3 x 3 =	21
4 x 3 =	9
5 x 3 =	30
6 x 3 =	15
7 x 3 =	27
8 x 3 =	33
9 x 3 =	12
10 x 3 =	36
11 x 3 =	3
12 x 3 =	18

Now write out the three times table up to ten times three, as quickly as you can. Write one line at a time and say it as you write it.

Now keep practising!

Three Times Table

OHP Display

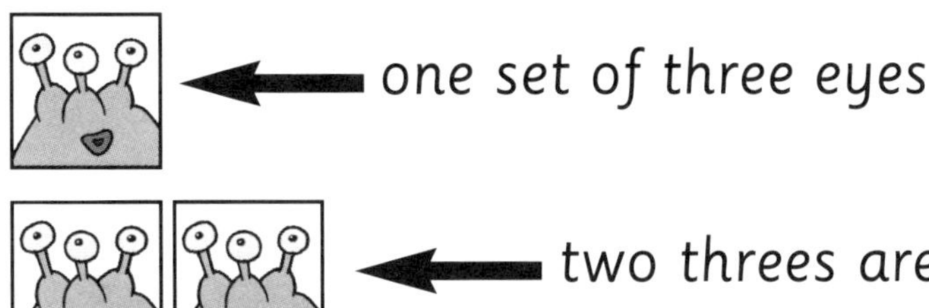

one set of three eyes

two threes are six

three threes are nine

four threes are twelve

five threes are fifteen

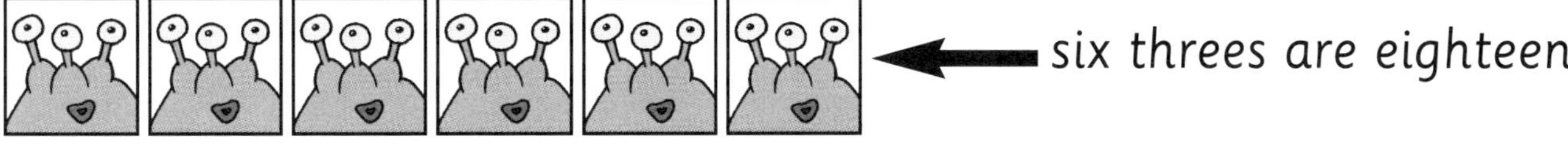

six threes are eighteen

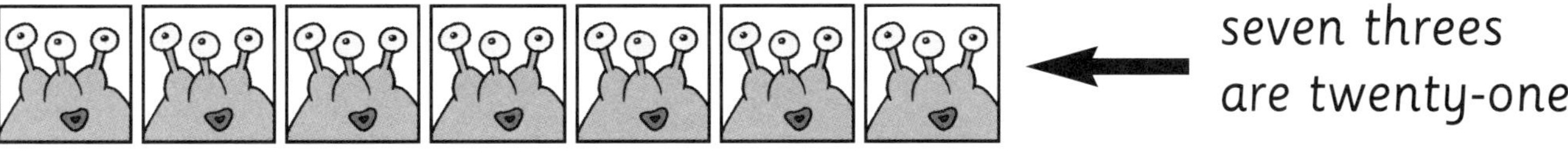

seven threes are twenty-one

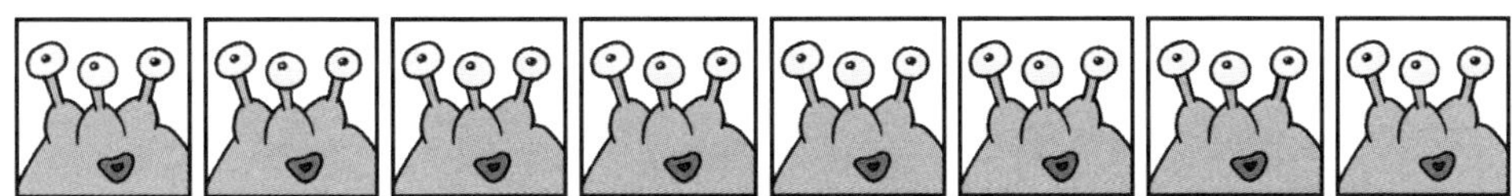

eight threes are twenty-four

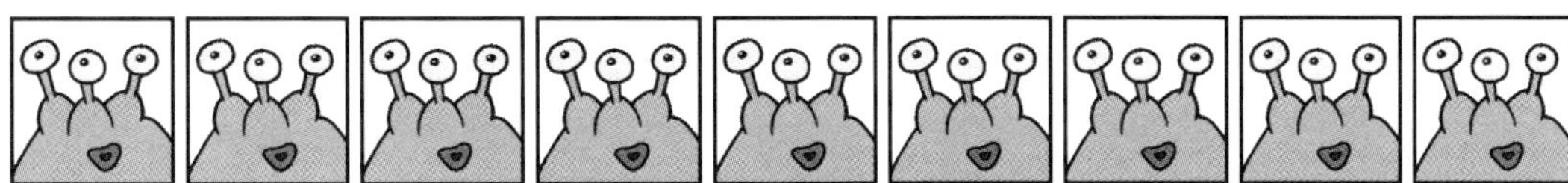

nine threes are twenty-seven

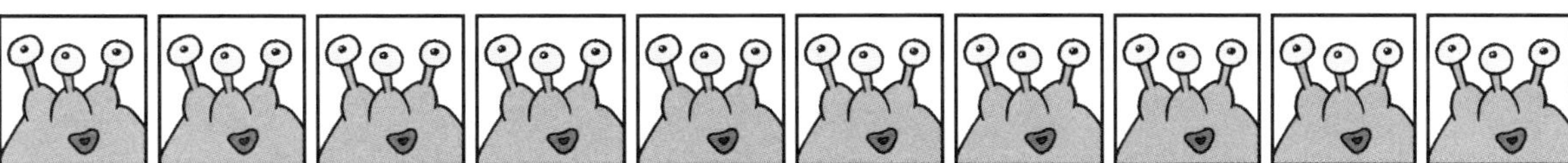

ten threes are thirty

Three Times Table

Worksheet Name: Date:

1	2	3	4	5	6
7	8	9	10	11	12
13	14	15	16	17	18
19	20	21	22	23	24
25	26	27	28	29	30
31	32	33	34	35	36

Now shade the multiples of two like this: 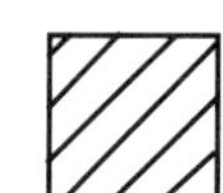

Which numbers are multiples of two and three? ☐ ☐ ☐ ☐ ☐ ☐

Four Times Table

OHP Display A

1 x 4 = 4

2 x 4 = 8

3 x 4 = 12

4 x 4 = 16

5 x 4 = 20

6 x 4 = 24

7 x 4 = 28

8 x 4 = 32

9 x 4 = 36

10 x 4 = 40

11 x 4 = 44

12 x 4 = 48

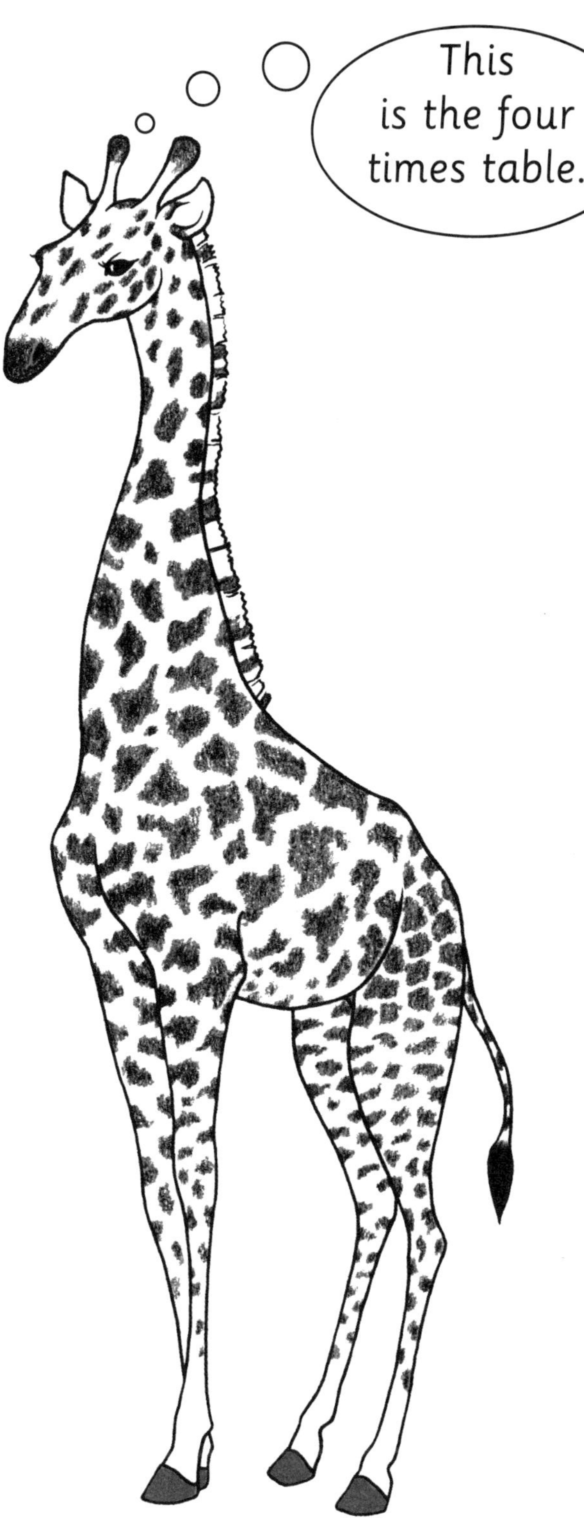

Look:

0 x 4 = 0

Four Times Table

OHP Display B

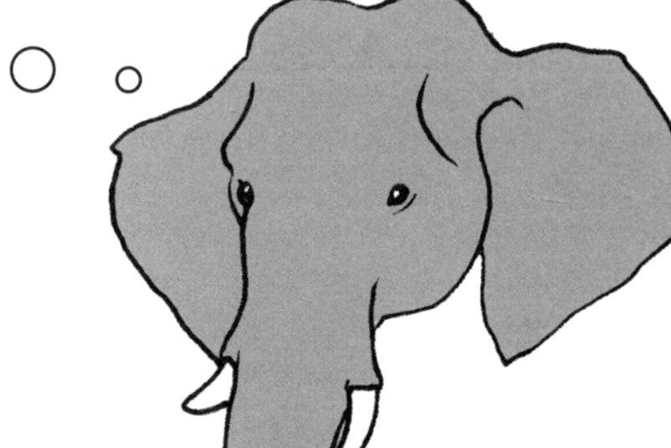

One times four is four.	1 x 4 = 4
Two fours are eight.	2 x 4 = 8
Three fours are twelve.	3 x 4 = 12
Four fours are sixteen.	4 x 4 = 16
Five fours are twenty.	5 x 4 = 20
Six fours are twenty-four.	6 x 4 = 24
Seven fours are twenty-eight.	7 x 4 = 28
Eight fours are thirty-two.	8 x 4 = 32
Nine fours are thirty-six.	9 x 4 = 36
Ten fours are forty.	10 x 4 = 40

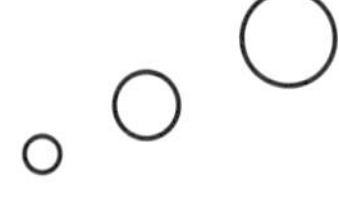

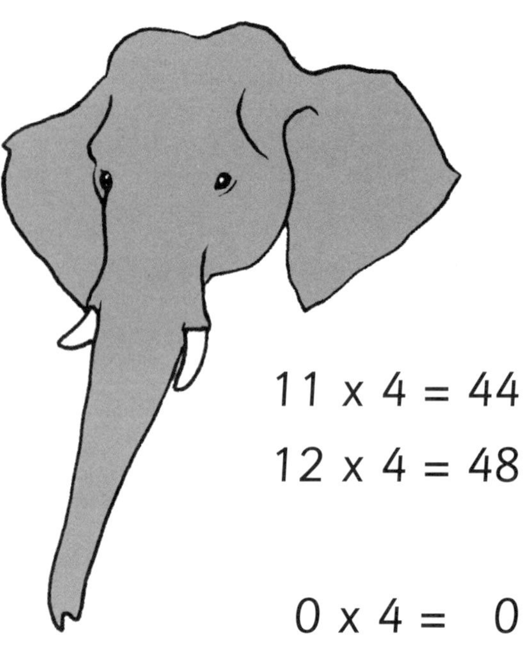

Eleven fours are forty-four.	11 x 4 = 44
Twelve fours are forty-eight.	12 x 4 = 48
Don't forget this one:	
Zero times four is zero.	0 x 4 = 0

Four Times Table

Worksheet Name: Date:

Keep saying the four times table.

If you say it four times every day it gets easier.

Fill in all the gaps of this four times table.

1 x 4 = ☐
__ __ __ __ ☐
__ __ __ __ ☐
4 x 4 = 16
__ __ __ __ ☐
__ __ __ __ ☐
__ __ __ __ ☐
8 x 4 = 32
__ __ __ __ ☐
__ __ __ __ ☐
__ __ __ __ ☐
12 x 4 = 48

Match the questions to the answers.

0 x 4 =	24
1 x 4 =	8
2 x 4 =	0
3 x 4 =	20
4 x 4 =	16
5 x 4 =	28
6 x 4 =	40
7 x 4 =	48
8 x 4 =	36
9 x 4 =	12
10 x 4 =	32
11 x 4 =	4
12 x 4 =	44

Now write out the four times table up to ten times four, as quickly as you can. Write one line at a time and say it as you write it.

____
____
____
____
____
____
____
____
____
____

Now keep practising!

Four Times Table

Worksheet Name: Date:

Colour the multiples of four on a seven by seven grid.

Look at the pattern made by the four times table.

1	2	3	4	5	6	7
8	9	10	11	12	13	14
15	16	17	18	19	20	21
22	23	24	25	26	27	28
29	30	31	32	33	34	35
36	37	38	39	40	41	42

Now shade the multiples of three like this: 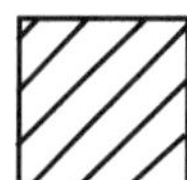

Which numbers are multiples of three and four ? ☐ ☐ ☐

Five Times Table

OHP Display A

1 x 5 = 5

2 x 5 = 10

3 x 5 = 15

4 x 5 = 20

5 x 5 = 25

6 x 5 = 30

7 x 5 = 35

8 x 5 = 40

9 x 5 = 45

10 x 5 = 50

11 x 5 = 55

12 x 5 = 60

This is the five times table.

You need to learn it.

Look:

0 x 5 = 0

Five Times Table

OHP Display B

This is the five times table.

One times five is five.	1 x 5 = 5
Two fives are ten.	2 x 5 = 10
Three fives are fifteen.	3 x 5 = 15
Four fives are twenty.	4 x 5 = 20
Five fives are twenty-five.	5 x 5 = 25
Six fives are thirty.	6 x 5 = 30
Seven fives are thirty-five.	7 x 5 = 35
Eight fives are forty.	8 x 5 = 40
Nine fives are forty-five.	9 x 5 = 45
Ten fives are fifty.	10 x 5 = 50

Some people like to learn eleven times five and twelve times five.

Eleven fives are fifty-five.	11 x 5 = 55
Twelve fives are sixty.	12 x 5 = 60

Don't forget this one:

Zero times five is zero.	0 x 5 = 0

Five Times Table

Worksheet Name: Date:

Fill in all the gaps.

1 x 5 = ☐
2 x 5 = ☐
___ ___ ___ ___ ☐
___ ___ ___ ___ ☐
___ ___ ___ ___ ☐
___ ___ ___ ___ ☐
___ ___ ___ ___ ☐
___ ___ ___ ___ ☐
9 x 5 = 45
___ ___ ___ ___ ☐
___ ___ ___ ___ ☐
___ ___ ___ ☐

Match the questions to the answers.

0 x 5 =	55
1 x 5 =	10
2 x 5 =	0
3 x 5 =	25
4 x 5 =	40
5 x 5 =	20
6 x 5 =	15
7 x 5 =	50
8 x 5 =	30
9 x 5 =	35
10 x 5 =	60
11 x 5 =	5
12 x 5 =	45

Now write out the five times table up to ten times five, as quickly as you can. Write one line at a time and say it as you write it.

____
____
____
____
____
____
____
____
____
____

Now keep practising!

Five Times Table

Worksheet Name: Date:

Colour in all the multiples of five on the eight by eight grid.

Does the five times table make a pattern?

1	2	3	4	5	6	7	8
9	10	11	12	13	14	15	16
17	18	19	20	21	22	23	24
25	26	27	28	29	30	31	32
33	34	35	36	37	38	39	40
41	42	43	44	45	46	47	48
49	50	51	52	53	54	55	56
57	58	59	60	61	62	63	64

Now shade the multiples of four like this:

Which numbers are multiples of four and five ?

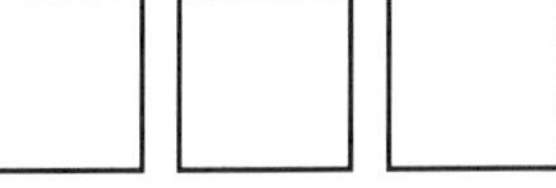

Six Times Table

OHP Display A

1 x 6 = 6

2 x 6 = 12

3 x 6 = 18

4 x 6 = 24

5 x 6 = 30

6 x 6 = 36

7 x 6 = 42

8 x 6 = 48

9 x 6 = 54

10 x 6 = 60

11 x 6 = 66

12 x 6 = 72

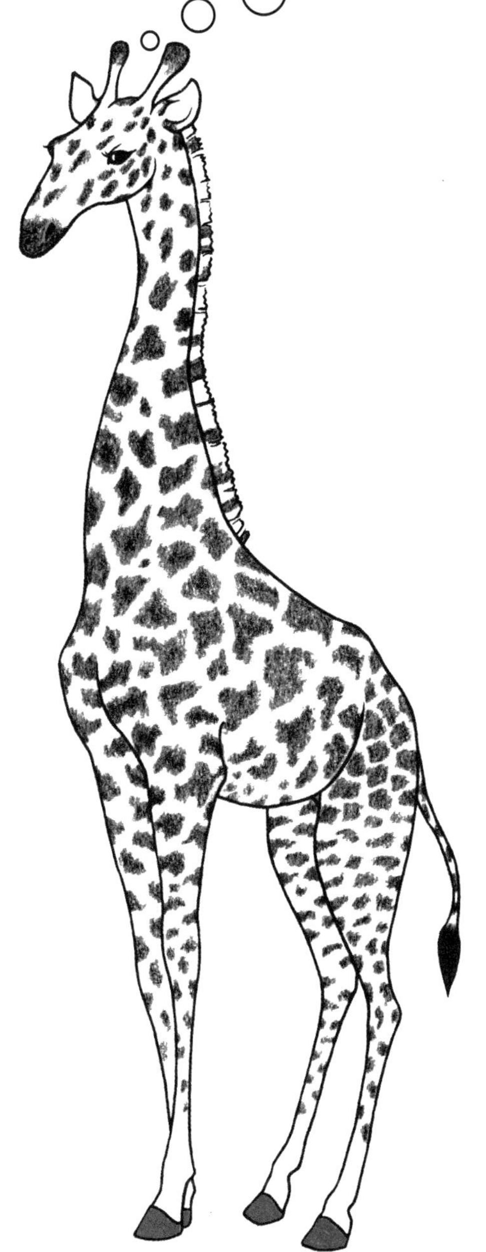

Look:

0 x 6 = 0

Six Times Table

OHP Display B

Keep saying the six times table.

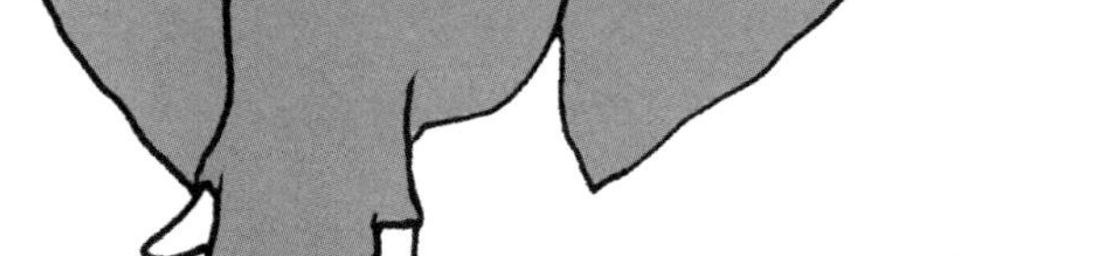

One times six is six.	1 x 6 = 6
Two sixes are twelve.	2 x 6 = 12
Three sixes are eighteen.	3 x 6 = 18
Four sixes are twenty-four.	4 x 6 = 24
Five sixes are thirty.	5 x 6 = 30
Six sixes are thirty-six.	6 x 6 = 36
Seven sixes are forty-two.	7 x 6 = 42
Eight sixes are forty-eight.	8 x 6 = 48
Nine sixes are fifty-four.	9 x 6 = 54
Ten sixes are sixty.	10 x 6 = 60

Some people like to learn eleven times six and twelve times six.

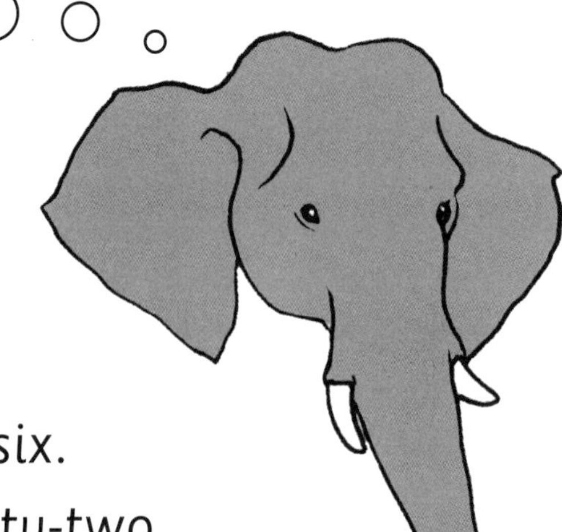

Eleven sixes are sixty-six.	11 x 6 = 66
Twelve sixes are seventy-two.	12 x 6 = 72
Don't forget this one:	
Zero times six is zero.	0 x 6 = 0

Six Times Table

Worksheet Name: Date:

Keep saying the six times table.

Fill in all the gaps.

0 x 6 = ☐
1 x 6 = ☐
__ __ __ __ ☐
__ __ __ __ ☐
__ __ __ __ ☐
5 x 6 = ☐
__ __ __ __ ☐
__ __ __ __ ☐
__ __ __ __ ☐
__ __ __ __ ☐
__ __ __ __ ☐
__ __ __ __ ☐
__ __ __ __ ☐

Match the questions to the answers.

0 x 6 =	48
1 x 6 =	12
2 x 6 =	0
3 x 6 =	42
4 x 6 =	18
5 x 6 =	60
6 x 6 =	30
7 x 6 =	54
8 x 6 =	66
9 x 6 =	24
10 x 6 =	72
11 x 6 =	6
12 x 6 =	36

Now write out the six times table up to ten times six, as quickly as you can. Write one line at a time and say it as you write it.

Now keep practising!

Six Times Table

Worksheet Name: Date:

Colour in all the multiples of six on the nine by nine grid.

Look for the pattern.

1	2	3	4	5	6	7	8	9
10	11	12	13	14	15	16	17	18
19	20	21	22	23	24	25	26	27
28	29	30	31	32	33	34	35	36
37	38	39	40	41	42	43	44	45
46	47	48	49	50	51	52	53	54
55	56	57	58	59	60	61	62	63
64	65	66	67	68	69	70	71	72
73	74	75	76	77	78	79	80	81

Now shade the multiples of four like this:

Which numbers are multiples of four and six ?

Seven Times Table

OHP Display A

1 x 7 = 7

2 x 7 = 14

3 x 7 = 21

4 x 7 = 28

5 x 7 = 35

6 x 7 = 42

7 x 7 = 49

8 x 7 = 56

9 x 7 = 63

10 x 7 = 70

11 x 7 = 77

12 x 7 = 84

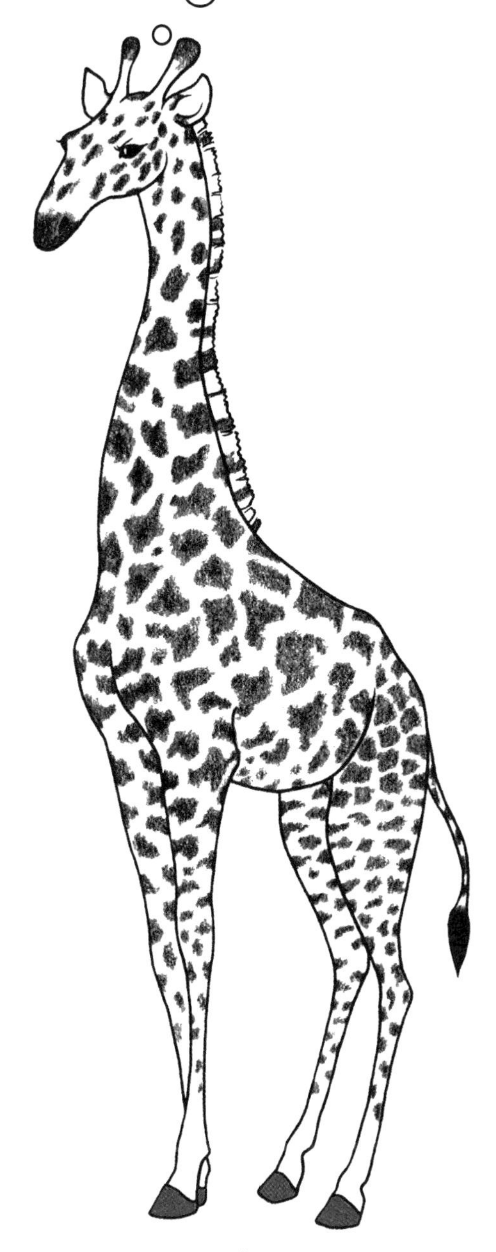

Look:

0 x 7 = 0

Seven Times Table

OHP Display B

Keep saying the seven times table.

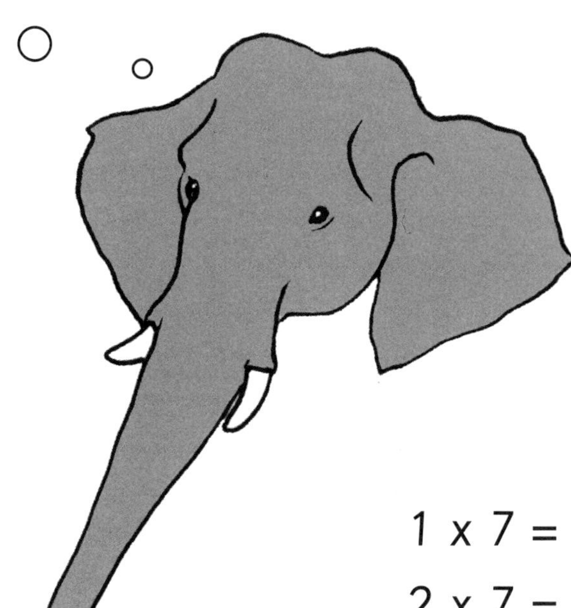

One times seven is seven. 1 x 7 = 7

Two sevens are fourteen. 2 x 7 = 14

Three sevens are twenty-one. 3 x 7 = 21

Four sevens are twenty-eight. 4 x 7 = 28

Five sevens are thirty-five. 5 x 7 = 35

Six sevens are forty-two. 6 x 7 = 42

Seven sevens are forty-nine. 7 x 7 = 49

Eight sevens are fifty-six. 8 x 7 = 56

Nine sevens are sixty-three. 9 x 7 = 63

Ten sevens are seventy. 10 x 7 = 70

Eleven sevens are seventy-seven. 11 x 7 = 77

Twelve sevens are eighty-four. 12 x 7 = 84

Don't forget this one:

Zero times seven is zero. 0 x 7 = 0

Seven Times Table

Worksheet Name: Date:

Say the seven times table just three times every day.

Do this for a week and you will begin to remember it!

Fill in all the gaps.

0 x 7 = ☐

1 x 7 = 7

2 x 7 = ☐

__ __ __ __ ☐

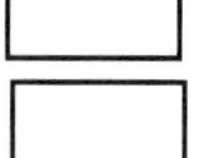

__ __ __ __ ☐

5 x 7 = ☐

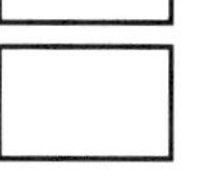

__ __ __ __ ☐

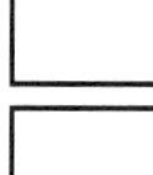

__ __ __ __ ☐

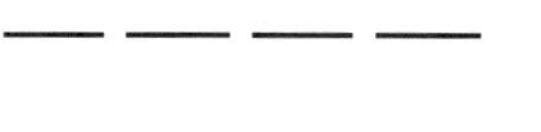

__ __ __ __ ☐

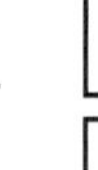

__ __ __ __ ☐

__ __ __ __ ☐

__ __ __ __ ☐

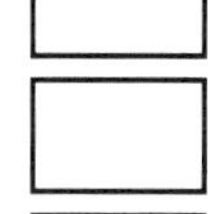

__ __ __ __ ☐

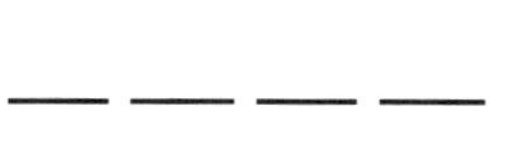

__ __ __ __ ☐

Match the questions to the answers.

0 x 7 =	77
1 x 7 =	14
2 x 7 =	0
3 x 7 =	70
4 x 7 =	49
5 x 7 =	28
6 x 7 =	21
7 x 7 =	56
8 x 7 =	42
9 x 7 =	35
10 x 7 =	84
11 x 7 =	7
12 x 7 =	63

Now write out the seven times table up to ten times seven, as quickly as you can.

Write one line at a time and say it as you write it.

____

____

____

____

____

____

____

____

____

____

Now keep practising!

Seven Times Table

Worksheet

Name:

Date:

Colour in all the multiples of seven on the ten by ten grid.

Then shade in all multiples of three.

1	2	3	4	5	6	7	8	9	10
11	12	13	14	15	16	17	18	19	20
21	22	23	24	25	26	27	28	29	30
31	32	33	34	35	36	37	38	39	40
41	42	43	44	45	46	47	48	49	50
51	52	53	54	55	56	57	58	59	60
61	62	63	64	65	66	67	68	69	70
71	72	73	74	75	76	77	78	79	80
81	82	83	84	85	86	87	88	89	90
91	92	93	94	95	96	97	98	99	100

Write all the multiples of three that are on the grid and are greater than 36.

Which numbers are multiples of three and seven?

Eight Times Table

OHP Display A

1 x 8 = 8

2 x 8 = 16

3 x 8 = 24

4 x 8 = 32

5 x 8 = 40

6 x 8 = 48

7 x 8 = 56

8 x 8 = 64

9 x 8 = 72

10 x 8 = 80

11 x 8 = 88

12 x 8 = 96

Look:

0 x 8 = 0

Eight Times Table

OHP Display B

One times eight is eight.	1 x 8 = 8
Two eights are sixteen.	2 x 8 = 16
Three eights are twenty-four.	3 x 8 = 24
Four eights are thirty-two.	4 x 8 = 32
Five eights are forty.	5 x 8 = 40
Six eights are forty-eight.	6 x 8 = 48
Seven eights are fifty-six.	7 x 8 = 56
Eight eights are sixty-four.	8 x 8 = 64
Nine eights are seventy-two.	9 x 8 = 72
Ten eights are eighty.	10 x 8 = 80
Eleven eights are eighty-eight.	11 x 8 = 88
Twelve eights are ninety-six.	12 x 8 = 96

Don't forget this one:

Zero times eight is zero.	0 x 8 = 0

Eight Times Table

Worksheet Name: Date:

Some people find 'seven times eight' a difficult bit to remember.

Seven eights are fifty-six.

Fill in all the gaps.

0 x 8 = ☐
1 x 8 = 8
2 x 8 = ☐
___ ___ ___ ___ ☐
___ ___ ___ ___ ☐
5 x 8 = ☐
___ ___ ___ ___ ☐

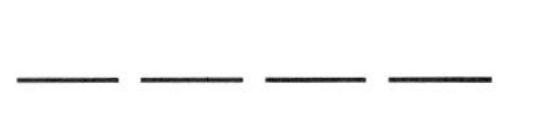

Match the questions to the answers.

0 x 8 =	88
1 x 8 =	16
2 x 8 =	0
3 x 8 =	80
4 x 8 =	56
5 x 8 =	32
6 x 8 =	24
7 x 8 =	64
8 x 8 =	48
9 x 8 =	40
10 x 8 =	96
11 x 8 =	8
12 x 8 =	72

Now write out the eight times table up to ten times eight, as quickly as you can. Write one line at a time and say it as you write it.

Now keep practising!

Eight Times Table

Worksheet Name: Date:

Colour in all the multiples of eight on the ten by ten grid.

Then shade in all multiples of six.

1	2	3	4	5	6	7	8	9	10
11	12	13	14	15	16	17	18	19	20
21	22	23	24	25	26	27	28	29	30
31	32	33	34	35	36	37	38	39	40
41	42	43	44	45	46	47	48	49	50
51	52	53	54	55	56	57	58	59	60
61	62	63	64	65	66	67	68	69	70
71	72	73	74	75	76	77	78	79	80
81	82	83	84	85	86	87	88	89	90
91	92	93	94	95	96	97	98	99	100

Which multiples of six that are on the grid are greater than 72?

☐ ☐ ☐ ☐

Which numbers are multiples of six and eight? ☐ ☐ ☐ ☐

Nine Times Table

OHP Display A

1 x 9 = 9

2 x 9 = 18

3 x 9 = 27

4 x 9 = 36

5 x 9 = 45

6 x 9 = 54

7 x 9 = 63

8 x 9 = 72

9 x 9 = 81

10 x 9 = 90

11 x 9 = 99

12 x 9 = 108

Look:

0 x 9 = 0

Nine Times Table

OHP Display B

Keep saying the nine times table.

One times nine is nine. 1 x 9 = 9

Two nines are eighteen. 2 x 9 = 18

Three nines are twenty-seven. 3 x 9 = 27

Four nines are thirty-six. 4 x 9 = 36

Five nines are forty-five. 5 x 9 = 45

Six nines are fifty-four. 6 x 9 = 54

Seven nines are sixty-three. 7 x 9 = 63

Eight nines are seventy-two. 8 x 9 = 72

Nine nines are eighty-one. 9 x 9 = 81

Ten nines are ninety. 10 x 9 = 90

Some people like to learn eleven times nine and twelve times nine.

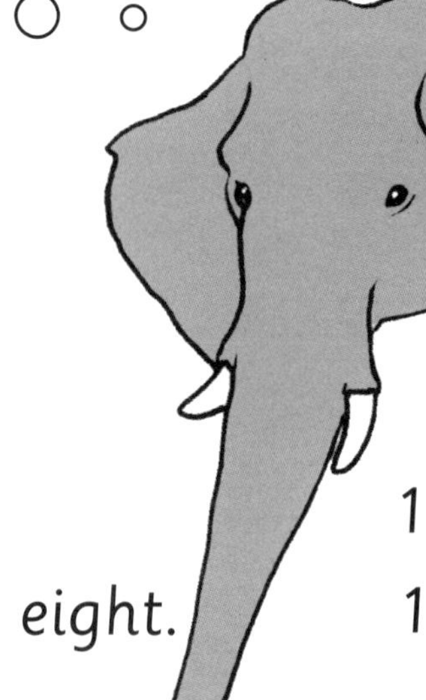

Eleven nines are ninety-nine. 11 x 9 = 99

Twelve nines are one hundred and eight. 12 x 9 = 108

Don't forget this one:

Zero times nine is zero. 0 x 9 = 0

Nine Times Table

Worksheet Name: Date:

Fill in all the gaps.

0 x 9 = ☐
1 x 9 = ☐
____ ____ ____ ____ ☐
____ ____ ____ ____ ☐
____ ____ ____ ____ ☐
5 x 9 = ☐
6 x 9 = ☐
____ ____ ____ ____ ☐
____ ____ ____ ____ ☐
9 x 9 = ☐
____ ____ ____ ____ ☐
____ ____ ____ ____ ☐
____ ____ ____ ____ ☐

Match the questions to the answers.

0 x 9 =	27
1 x 9 =	45
2 x 9 =	0
3 x 9 =	18
4 x 9 =	63
5 x 9 =	90
6 x 9 =	9
7 x 9 =	36
8 x 9 =	99
9 x 9 =	54
10 x 9 =	72
11 x 9 =	108
12 x 9 =	81

Now write out the nine times table up to ten times nine, as quickly as you can. Write one line at a time and say it as you write it.

Now keep practising!

Nine Times Table

Worksheet Name: Date:

Colour in all the multiples of nine on the ten by ten grid.

Then shade the multiples of seven.

1	2	3	4	5	6	7	8	9	10
11	12	13	14	15	16	17	18	19	20
21	22	23	24	25	26	27	28	29	30
31	32	33	34	35	36	37	38	39	40
41	42	43	44	45	46	47	48	49	50
51	52	53	54	55	56	57	58	59	60
61	62	63	64	65	66	67	68	69	70
71	72	73	74	75	76	77	78	79	80
81	82	83	84	85	86	87	88	89	90
91	92	93	94	95	96	97	98	99	100

What would be the next multiple of nine? ☐

What is the only multiple of both seven and nine that appears on the grid? ☐

Ten Times Table

OHP Display A

1 x 10 = 10

2 x 10 = 20

3 x 10 = 30

4 x 10 = 40

5 x 10 = 50

6 x 10 = 60

7 x 10 = 70

8 x 10 = 80

9 x 10 = 90

10 x 10 = 100

11 x 10 = 110

12 x 10 = 120

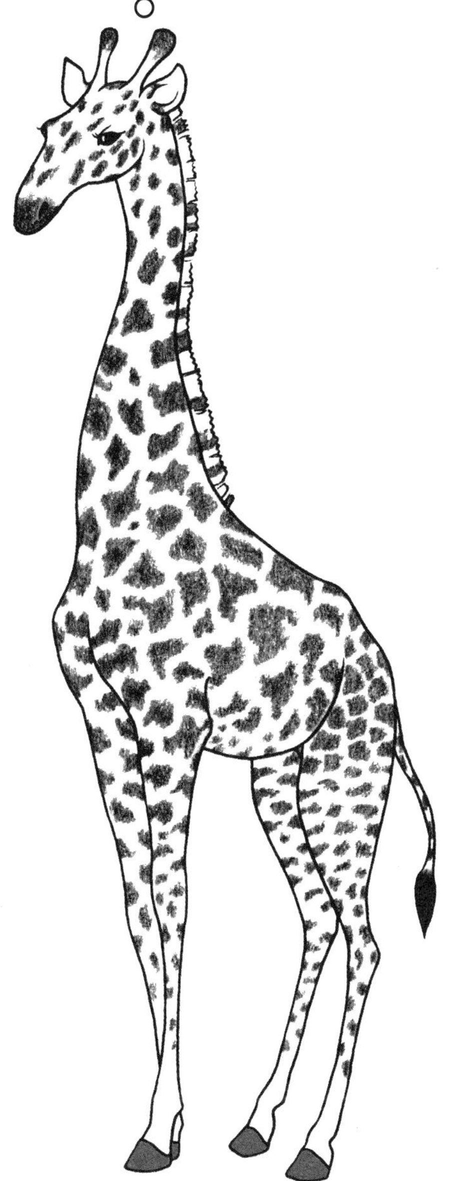

Look:

0 x 10 = 0

Ten Times Table

OHP Display B

Keep saying the ten times table.

One times ten is ten.	1 x 10 = 10
Two tens are twenty.	2 x 10 = 20
Three tens are thirty.	3 x 10 = 30
Four tens are forty.	4 x 10 = 40
Five tens are fifty.	5 x 10 = 50
Six tens are sixty.	6 x 10 = 60
Seven tens are seventy.	7 x 10 = 70
Eight tens are eighty.	8 x 10 = 80
Nine tens are ninety.	9 x 10 = 90
Ten tens are one hundred.	10 x 10 = 100

Some people like to learn eleven times ten and twelve times ten.

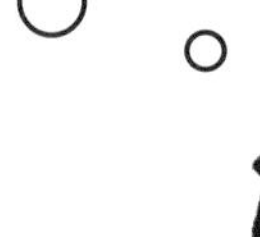

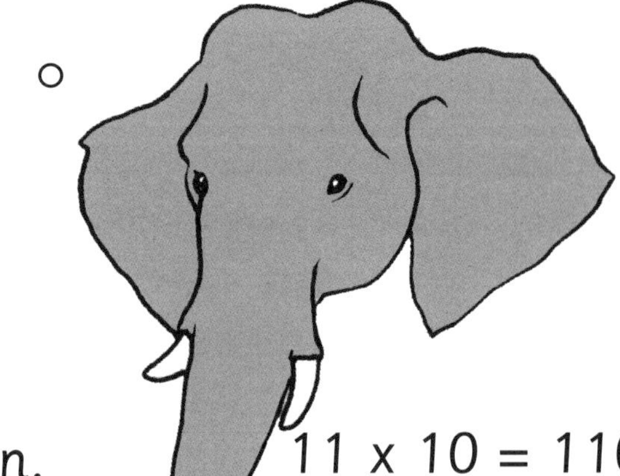

Eleven tens are one hundred and ten.	11 x 10 = 110
Twelve tens are one hundred and twenty.	12 x 10 = 120
Don't forget this one:	
Zero times ten is zero.	0 x 10 = 0

Ten Times Table

Worksheet Name: Date:

All multiples of ten … … end with a zero.

Fill in all the gaps.

0 x 10 = [ ]
__ __ __ __ [ ]
__ __ __ __ [ ]
__ __ __ __ [ ]
__ __ __ __ [ ]
5 x 10 = [ ]
__ __ __ __ [ ]
__ __ __ __ [ ]
__ __ __ __ [ ]
__ __ __ __ [ ]
__ __ __ __ [ ]
__ __ __ __ [ ]
12 x 10 = [ ]
13 x 10 = [ ]
14 x 10 = [ ]
15 x 10 = [ ]
16 x 10 = [ ]
17 x 10 = [ ]
18 x 10 = [ ]
19 x 10 = [ ]
20 x 10 = [ ]
25 x 10 = [ ]

Match the questions to the answers.

0 x 10 =	20
1 x 10 =	40
2 x 10 =	10
3 x 10 =	90
4 x 10 =	60
5 x 10 =	100
6 x 10 =	30
7 x 10 =	80
8 x 10 =	110
9 x 10 =	70
10 x 10 =	120
11 x 10 =	0
12 x 10 =	50

Now write out the ten times table.

Ten Times Table

Worksheet Name: Date:

1	2	3	4	5	6	7	8
9	10	11	12	13	14	15	16
17	18	19	20	21	22	23	24
25	26	27	28	29	30	31	32
33	34	35	36	37	38	39	40
41	42	43	44	45	46	47	48
49	50	51	52	53	54	55	56
57	58	59	60	61	62	63	64

1	2	3	4	5	6	7	8	9
10	11	12	13	14	15	16	17	18
19	20	21	22	23	24	25	26	27
28	29	30	31	32	33	34	35	36
37	38	39	40	41	42	43	44	45
46	47	48	49	50	51	52	53	54
55	56	57	58	59	60	61	62	63
64	65	66	67	68	69	70	71	72
73	74	75	76	77	78	79	80	81

Colour the multiples of ten on all of these grids. Look how the pattern changes.

1	2	3	4	5	6	7	8	9	10
11	12	13	14	15	16	17	18	19	20
21	22	23	24	25	26	27	28	29	30
31	32	33	34	35	36	37	38	39	40
41	42	43	44	45	46	47	48	49	50
51	52	53	54	55	56	57	58	59	60
61	62	63	64	65	66	67	68	69	70
71	72	73	74	75	76	77	78	79	80
81	82	83	84	85	86	87	88	89	90
91	92	93	94	95	96	97	98	99	100

Eleven Times Table

OHP Display A

1 x 11 = 11
2 x 11 = 22
3 x 11 = 33
4 x 11 = 44
5 x 11 = 55
6 x 11 = 66
7 x 11 = 77
8 x 11 = 88
9 x 11 = 99
10 x 11 = 110
11 x 11 = 121
12 x 11 = 132

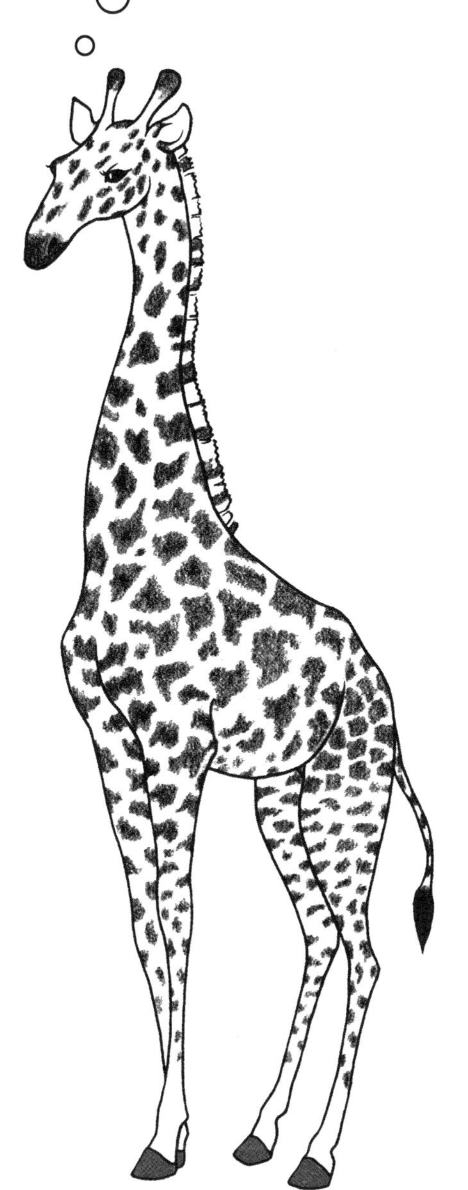

Look:
0 x 11 = 0

Eleven Times Table

OHP Display B

Keep saying the eleven times table.

One times eleven is eleven.	1 x 11 = 11
Two elevens are twenty-two.	2 x 11 = 22
Three elevens are thirty-three.	3 x 11 = 33
Four elevens are forty-four.	4 x 11 = 44
Five elevens are fifty-five.	5 x 11 = 55
Six elevens are sixty-six.	6 x 11 = 66
Seven elevens are seventy-seven.	7 x 11 = 77
Eight elevens are eighty-eight.	8 x 11 = 88
Nine elevens are ninety-nine.	9 x 11 = 99
Ten elevens are one hundred and ten.	10 x 11 = 110
Eleven elevens are one hundred and twenty-one.	11 x 11 = 121
Twelve elevens are one hundred and thirty-two.	12 x 11 = 132

Don't forget this one:

Zero times eleven is zero. 0 x 11 = 0

Eleven Times Table

Worksheet

Name:

Date:

The difficult bits of the eleven times table …

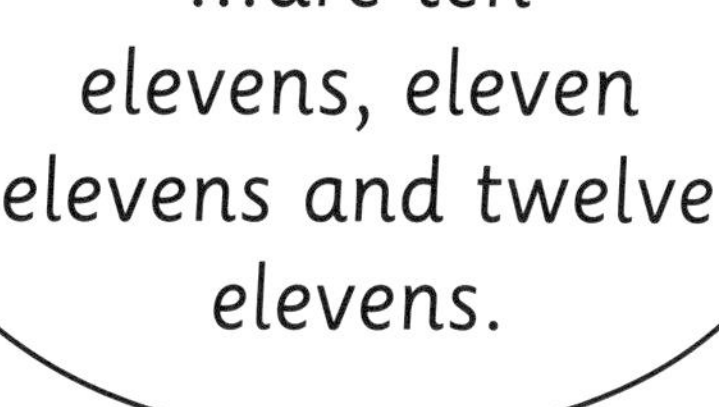

Fill in all the gaps.

0 x 11 =

1 x 11 =

____

____

____

5 x 11 =

____

____

____

____

10 x11 =

11 x11 =

12 x11 =

Match the questions to the answers.

0 x 11 =	33
1 x 11 =	55
2 x 11 =	132
3 x 11 =	22
4 x 11 =	99
5 x 11 =	88
6 x 11 =	11
7 x 11 =	44
8 x 11 =	121
9 x 11 =	66
10 x 11 =	77
11 x 11 =	110
12 x 11 =	0

Now write out the eleven times table up to ten times eleven, as quickly as you can. Write one line at a time and say it as you write it.

Now keep practising!

Eleven Times Table

Worksheet Name: Date:

Colour in the multiples of eleven.

1	2	3	4	5	6	7	8	9	10	11
12	13	14	15	16	17	18	19	20	21	22
23	24	25	26	27	28	29	30	31	32	33
34	35	36	37	38	39	40	41	42	43	44
45	46	47	48	49	50	51	52	53	54	55
56	57	58	59	60	61	62	63	64	65	66
67	68	69	70	71	72	73	74	75	76	77
78	79	80	81	82	83	84	85	86	87	88
89	90	91	92	93	94	95	96	97	98	99
100	101	102	103	104	105	106	107	108	109	110
111	112	113	114	115	116	117	118	119	120	121

Now put a cross X on all the multiples of two and draw a circle ○ on all the multiples of three. Which number is coloured and has a cross and a circle?

☐

Twelve Times Table

OHP Display A

1 x 12 = 12

2 x 12 = 24

3 x 12 = 36

4 x 12 = 48

5 x 12 = 60

6 x 12 = 72

7 x 12 = 84

8 x 12 = 96

9 x 12 = 108

10 x 12 = 120

11 x 12 = 132

12 x 12 = 144

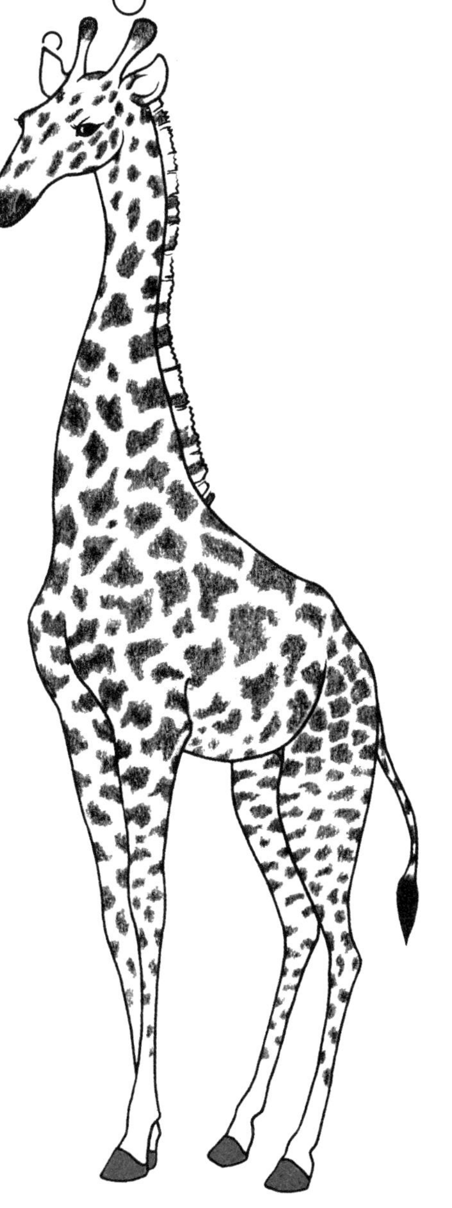

Look:

0 x 12 = 0

Twelve Times Table

OHP Display B

One times twelve is twelve.	1 x 12 = 12
Two twelves are twenty-four.	2 x 12 = 24
Three twelves are thirty-six.	3 x 12 = 36
Four twelves are forty-eight.	4 x 12 = 48
Five twelves are sixty.	5 x 12 = 60
Six twelves are seventy-two.	6 x 12 = 72
Seven twelves are eighty-four.	7 x 12 = 84
Eight twelves are ninety-six.	8 x 12 = 96
Nine twelves are one hundred and eight.	9 x 12 = 108
Ten twelves are one hundred and twenty.	10 x 12 = 120

Eleven twelves are one hundred and thirty-two.	11 x 12 = 132
Twelve twelves are one hundred and forty-four.	12 x 12 = 144

Don't forget this one:

Zero times twelve is zero.	0 x 12 = 0

Twelve Times Table

Worksheet Name: Date:

We learn the twelve times table just for fun.

Do you call this fun?

Fill in all the gaps.

0 x 12 = ☐
1 x 12 = ☐
__ __ __ __ ☐
__ __ __ __ ☐
__ __ __ __ ☐
5 x 12 = ☐
__ __ __ __ ☐
__ __ __ __ ☐
__ __ __ __ ☐
__ __ __ __ ☐
__ __ __ __ ☐
11 x 12 = ☐
12 x 12 = ☐

Match the questions to the answers.

0 x 12 =	96
1 x 12 =	48
2 x 12 =	60
3 x 12 =	24
4 x 12 =	84
5 x 12 =	144
6 x 12 =	108
7 x 12 =	12
8 x 12 =	120
9 x 12 =	36
10 x 12 =	132
11 x 12 =	72
12 x 12 =	0

Now write out the twelve times table up to ten times twelve, as quickly as you can. Write one line at a time and say it as you write it.

Now keep practising!

Twelve Times Table

Worksheet Name: Date:

Colour in the multiples of eleven.

That's too easy!

1	2	3	4	5	6	7	8	9	10	11	12
13	14	15	16	17	18	19	20	21	22	23	24
25	26	27	28	29	30	31	32	33	34	35	36
37	38	39	40	41	42	43	44	45	46	47	48
49	50	51	52	53	54	55	56	57	58	59	60
61	62	63	64	65	66	67	68	69	70	71	72
73	74	75	76	77	78	79	80	81	82	83	84
85	86	87	88	89	90	91	92	93	94	95	96
97	98	99	100	101	102	103	104	105	106	107	108
109	110	111	112	113	114	115	116	117	118	119	120
121	122	123	124	125	126	127	128	129	130	131	132
133	134	135	136	137	138	139	140	141	142	143	144

Now put a cross X on all multiples of five. Draw a circle ○ on all multiples of seven. Does any coloured square have a cross and a circle?

Twenty-five Times Table

OHP Display

1 x 25 = 25

2 x 25 = 50

3 x 25 = 75

4 x 25 = 100

5 x 25 = 125

6 x 25 = 150

7 x 25 = 175

8 x 25 = 200

9 x 25 = 225

10 x 25 = 250

11 x 25 = 275

12 x 25 = 300

Twenty-five Times Table

OHP Display

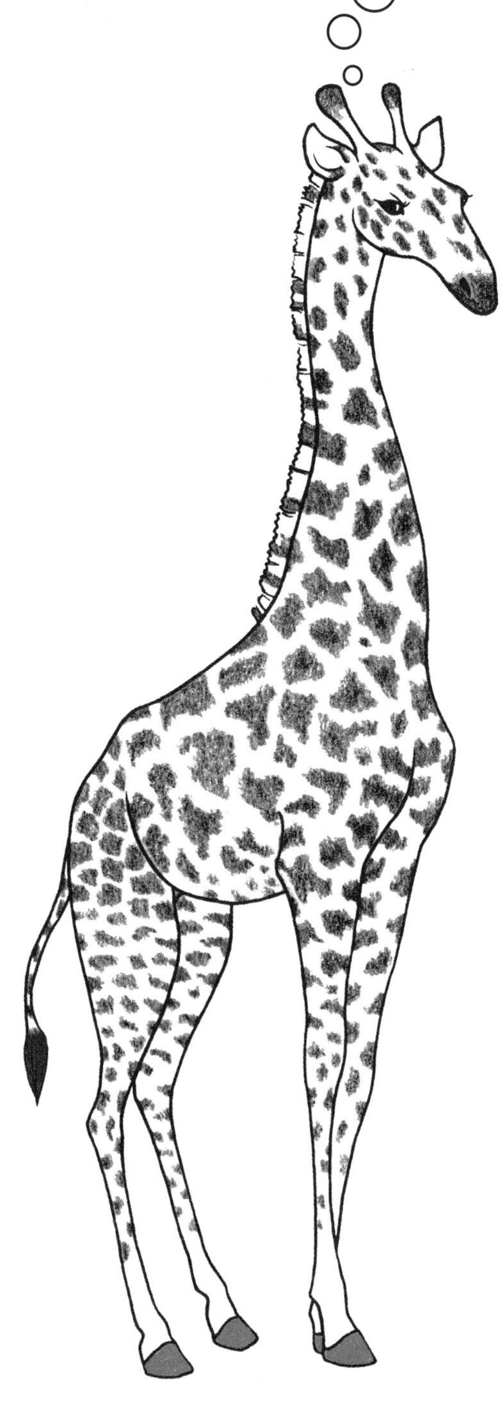

13 x 25 = 325

14 x 25 = 350

15 x 25 = 375

16 x 25 = 400

17 x 25 = 425

18 x 25 = 450

19 x 25 = 475

20 x 25 = 500

21 x 25 = 525

22 x 25 = 550

23 x 25 = 575

24 x 25 = 600

25 x 25 = 625

Times Tables

OHP Display

1 x 2 = 2
2 x 2 = 4
3 x 2 = 6
4 x 2 = 8
5 x 2 = 10
6 x 2 = 12
7 x 2 = 14
8 x 2 = 16
9 x 2 = 18
10 x 2 = 20

1 x 3 = 3
2 x 3 = 6
3 x 3 = 9
4 x 3 = 12
5 x 3 = 15
6 x 3 = 18
7 x 3 = 21
8 x 3 = 24
9 x 3 = 27
10 x 3 = 30

1 x 4 = 4
2 x 4 = 8
3 x 4 = 12
4 x 4 = 16
5 x 4 = 20
6 x 4 = 24
7 x 4 = 28
8 x 4 = 32
9 x 4 = 36
10 x 4 = 40

1 x 5 = 5
2 x 5 = 10
3 x 5 = 15
4 x 5 = 20
5 x 5 = 25
6 x 5 = 30
7 x 5 = 35
8 x 5 = 40
9 x 5 = 45
10 x 5 = 50

1 x 6 = 6
2 x 6 = 12
3 x 6 = 18
4 x 6 = 24
5 x 6 = 30
6 x 6 = 36
7 x 6 = 42
8 x 6 = 48
9 x 6 = 54
10 x 6 = 60

1 x 7 = 7
2 x 7= 14
3 x 7 = 21
4 x 7 = 28
5 x 7 = 35
6 x 7 = 42
7 x 7 = 49
8 x 7 = 56
9 x 7 = 63
10 x 7 = 70

1 x 8 = 8
2 x 8 = 16
3 x 8 = 24
4 x 8 = 32
5 x 8 = 40
6 x 8 = 48
7 x 8 = 56
8 x 8 = 64
9 x 8 = 72
10 x 8 = 80

1 x 9 = 9
2 x 9 = 18
3 x 9 = 27
4 x 9 = 36
5 x 9 = 45
6 x 9 = 54
7 x 9 = 63
8 x 9 = 72
9 x 9 = 81
10 x 9 = 90

1 x 10 = 10
2 x 10 = 20
3 x 10 = 30
4 x 10 = 40
5 x 10 = 50
6 x 10 = 60
7 x 10 = 70
8 x 10 = 80
9 x 10 = 90
10 x 10 =100

Multiplication (1)

Worksheet

Name: Date:

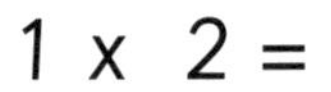

1 x 2 = ☐
2 x 2 = ☐
3 x 2 = ☐
4 x 2 = ☐
5 x 2 = ☐
6 x 2 = ☐
7 x 2 = ☐
8 x 2 = ☐
9 x 2 = ☐
10 x 2 = ☐

Time taken:
☐ seconds

1 x 3 = ☐
2 x 3 = ☐
3 x 3 = ☐
4 x 3 = ☐
5 x 3 = ☐
6 x 3 = ☐
7 x 3 = ☐
8 x 3 = ☐
9 x 3 = ☐
10 x 3 = ☐

Time taken:
☐ seconds

1 x 4 = ☐
2 x 4 = ☐
3 x 4 = ☐
4 x 4 = ☐
5 x 4 = ☐
6 x 4 = ☐
7 x 4 = ☐
8 x 4 = ☐
9 x 4 = ☐
10 x 4 = ☐

Time taken:
☐ seconds

1 x 5 = ☐
2 x 5 = ☐
3 x 5 = ☐
4 x 5 = ☐
5 x 5 = ☐
6 x 5 = ☐
7 x 5 = ☐
8 x 5 = ☐
9 x 5 = ☐
10 x 5 = ☐

Time taken:
☐ seconds

1 x 6 = ☐
2 x 6 = ☐
3 x 6 = ☐
4 x 6 = ☐
5 x 6 = ☐
6 x 6 = ☐
7 x 6 = ☐
8 x 6 = ☐
9 x 6 = ☐
10 x 6 = ☐

Time taken:
☐ seconds

1 x 7 = ☐
2 x 7 = ☐
3 x 7 = ☐
4 x 7 = ☐
5 x 7 = ☐
6 x 7 = ☐
7 x 7 = ☐
8 x 7 = ☐
9 x 7 = ☐
10 x 7 = ☐

Time taken:
☐ seconds

Multiplication (2)

Worksheet Name: Date:

How quickly can you answer all these questions?

Time yourself on each section.

1 x 8 =		1 x 9 =		1 x 10 =	
2 x 8 =		2 x 9 =		2 x 10 =	
3 x 8 =		3 x 9 =		3 x 10 =	
4 x 8 =		4 x 9 =		4 x 10 =	
5 x 8 =		5 x 9 =		5 x 10 =	
6 x 8 =		6 x 9 =		6 x 10 =	
7 x 8 =		7 x 9 =		7 x 10 =	
8 x 8 =		8 x 9 =		8 x 10 =	
9 x 8 =		9 x 9 =		9 x 10 =	
10 x 8 =		10 x 9 =		10 x 10 =	
Time taken: ___ seconds		Time taken: ___ seconds		Time taken: ___ seconds	

1 x 11 =		1 x 12 =		1 x 25 =	
2 x 11 =		2 x 12 =		2 x 25 =	
3 x 11 =		3 x 12 =		3 x 25 =	
4 x 11 =		4 x 12 =		4 x 25 =	
5 x 11 =		5 x 12 =		5 x 25 =	
6 x 11 =		6 x 12 =		6 x 25 =	
7 x 11 =		7 x 12 =		7 x 25 =	
8 x 11 =		8 x 12 =		8 x 25 =	
9 x 11 =		9 x 12 =		9 x 25 =	
10 x 11 =		10 x 12 =		10 x 25 =	
11 x 11 =		11 x 12 =		11 x 25 =	
12 x 11 =		12 x 12 =		12 x 25 =	
Time taken: ___ seconds		Time taken: ___ seconds		Time taken: ___ seconds	

Division (1)

Worksheet Name: Date:

How quickly can you answer these divisions?

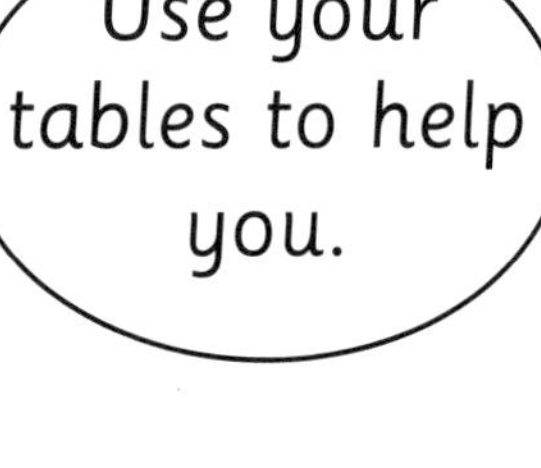

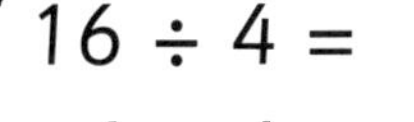

$14 \div 2 =$ ☐
$20 \div 2 =$ ☐
$4 \div 2 =$ ☐
$8 \div 2 =$ ☐
$12 \div 2 =$ ☐
$6 \div 2 =$ ☐
$2 \div 2 =$ ☐
$10 \div 2 =$ ☐
$16 \div 2 =$ ☐
$18 \div 2 =$ ☐

Time taken: ☐ seconds

$27 \div 3 =$ ☐
$18 \div 3 =$ ☐
$9 \div 3 =$ ☐
$15 \div 3 =$ ☐
$12 \div 3 =$ ☐
$6 \div 3 =$ ☐
$21 \div 3 =$ ☐
$3 \div 3 =$ ☐
$30 \div 3 =$ ☐
$24 \div 3 =$ ☐

Time taken: ☐ seconds

$16 \div 4 =$ ☐
$4 \div 4 =$ ☐
$24 \div 4 =$ ☐
$36 \div 4 =$ ☐
$8 \div 4 =$ ☐
$20 \div 4 =$ ☐
$40 \div 4 =$ ☐
$28 \div 4 =$ ☐
$12 \div 4 =$ ☐
$32 \div 4 =$ ☐

Time taken: ☐ seconds

$25 \div 5 =$ ☐
$10 \div 5 =$ ☐
$45 \div 5 =$ ☐
$5 \div 5 =$ ☐
$15 \div 5 =$ ☐
$30 \div 5 =$ ☐
$20 \div 5 =$ ☐
$50 \div 5 =$ ☐
$40 \div 5 =$ ☐
$35 \div 5 =$ ☐

Time taken: ☐ seconds

$30 \div 6 =$ ☐
$42 \div 6 =$ ☐
$54 \div 6 =$ ☐
$12 \div 6 =$ ☐
$24 \div 6 =$ ☐
$6 \div 6 =$ ☐
$60 \div 6 =$ ☐
$18 \div 6 =$ ☐
$36 \div 6 =$ ☐
$48 \div 6 =$ ☐

Time taken: ☐ seconds

$42 \div 7 =$ ☐
$21 \div 7 =$ ☐
$14 \div 7 =$ ☐
$49 \div 7 =$ ☐
$63 \div 7 =$ ☐
$28 \div 7 =$ ☐
$7 \div 7 =$ ☐
$35 \div 7 =$ ☐
$56 \div 7 =$ ☐
$70 \div 7 =$ ☐

Time taken: ☐ seconds

Division (2)

Worksheet Name: Date:

How quickly can you answer these divisions?

Use your tables to help you.

64 ÷ 8 = ☐
8 ÷ 8 = ☐
24 ÷ 8 = ☐
48 ÷ 8 = ☐
40 ÷ 8 = ☐
80 ÷ 8 = ☐
16 ÷ 8 = ☐
72 ÷ 8 = ☐
32 ÷ 8 = ☐
56 ÷ 8 = ☐

Time taken: ☐ seconds

72 ÷ 9 = ☐
27 ÷ 9 = ☐
9 ÷ 9 = ☐
45 ÷ 9 = ☐
81 ÷ 9 = ☐
18 ÷ 9 = ☐
90 ÷ 9 = ☐
36 ÷ 9 = ☐
54 ÷ 9 = ☐
63 ÷ 9 = ☐

Time taken: ☐ seconds

60 ÷ 10 = ☐
100 ÷ 10 = ☐
10 ÷ 10 = ☐
80 ÷ 10 = ☐
20 ÷ 10 = ☐
90 ÷ 10 = ☐
40 ÷ 10 = ☐
70 ÷ 10 = ☐
50 ÷ 10 = ☐
30 ÷ 10 = ☐

Time taken: ☐ seconds

55 ÷ 11 = ☐
121 ÷ 11 = ☐
66 ÷ 11 = ☐
22 ÷ 11 = ☐
99 ÷ 11 = ☐
11 ÷ 11 = ☐
132 ÷ 11 = ☐
77 ÷ 11 = ☐
33 ÷ 11 = ☐
88 ÷ 11 = ☐
44 ÷ 11 = ☐
110 ÷ 11 = ☐

Time taken:

seconds

96 ÷ 12 = ☐
132 ÷ 12 = ☐
48 ÷ 12 = ☐
60 ÷ 12 = ☐
12 ÷ 12 = ☐
108 ÷ 12 = ☐
72 ÷ 12 = ☐
120 ÷ 12 = ☐
36 ÷ 12 = ☐
84 ÷ 12 = ☐
144 ÷ 12 = ☐
24 ÷ 12 = ☐

Time taken: ☐ seconds

Multiplication Square

OHP Display

X	1	2	3	4	5	6	7	8	9	10	11	12
1	1	2	3	4	5	6	7	8	9	10	11	12
2	2	4	6	8	10	12	14	16	18	20	22	24
3	3	6	9	12	15	18	21	24	27	30	33	36
4	4	8	12	16	20	24	28	32	36	40	44	48
5	5	10	15	20	25	30	35	40	45	50	55	60
6	6	12	18	24	30	36	42	48	54	60	66	72
7	7	14	21	28	35	42	49	56	63	70	77	84
8	8	16	24	32	40	48	56	64	72	80	88	96
9	9	18	27	36	45	54	63	72	81	90	99	108
10	10	20	30	40	50	60	70	80	90	100	110	120
11	11	22	33	44	55	66	77	88	99	110	121	132
12	12	24	36	48	60	72	84	96	108	120	132	144

Empty Multiplication Square

Worksheet Name: Date:

How quickly can you fill in the answers?

Time yourself.

X	1	2	3	4	5	6	7	8	9	10	11	12
1												
2												
3												
4												
5												
6												
7												
8												
9												
10												
11												
12												

Time taken: ☐ minutes and ☐ seconds.

Mixed Multiplication Square (up to 10 x 10)

Worksheet

Name: Date:

Try to fill in the answers as quickly as you can.

X	9	3	10	1	4	5	2	7	8	6
3										
5										
7										
2										
1										
9										
8										
4										
10										
6										

Time taken: ☐ minutes and ☐ seconds.

Mixed Multiplication Square (up to 12 x 12)

Worksheet

Name:

Date:

Time yourself. It's tricky!

X	8	4	9	10	2	12	7	11	6	5	3	1
7												
5												
3												
1												
12												
11												
6												
4												
2												
10												
8												
9												

Time taken: ☐ minutes and ☐ seconds.

Make your own mix

Worksheet Name: Date:

X	1	2	3	4	5	6	7	8	9	10
1										
2										
3										
4										
5										
6										
7										
8										
9										
10										

X										

Make your own mix

Worksheet

Name:

Date:

X	1	2	3	4	5	6	7	8	9	10	11	12
1												
2												
3												
4												
5												
6												
7												
8												
9												
10												
11												
12												

X												

Mini-squares

Worksheet Name: Date:

X	6	2	4	3	5
5					
2					
3					
6					
4					

Time taken: ☐ seconds

X	7	4	6	8	5
4					
8					
6					
5					
7					

Time taken: ☐ seconds

X	9	7	8	10	12
7					
12					
9					
8					
10					

Time taken: ☐ seconds

X	3	6	5	4	2
8					
10					
7					
9					
12					

Time taken: ☐ seconds

X	100	50	25	75
4				
2				
3				
5				

Time taken: ☐ seconds

Multiples (1)

OHP Display

These numbers are multiples of six:

6 12 18 24 30 36 42 48 54 60 .....

There are lots more multiples of six. Here are some examples:

96 144 612 17172

Here are the multiples of four, up to 10 x 4:

4 8 12 16 20 24 28 32 36 40

Look again:

Multiples of six: 6 12 18 24 30 36 42 48 54 60

Multiples of four: 4 8 12 16 20 24 28 32 36 40

These numbers are in both lists: **12 24 36**

Multiples (2)

Worksheet Name: Date:

Write the multiples of three, up to 10 x 3:

Write the multiples of five, up to 10 x 5:

What is the Lowest Common Multiple of three and five?

Write the multiples of seven, up to 10 x 7:

What is the Lowest Common Multiple of three and seven?

What is the Lowest Common Multiple of five and seven?

Write the multiples of two, up to 10 x 2:

What is the Lowest Common Multiple of two and three?

What is the Lowest Common Multiple of two and five?

What is the Lowest Common Multiple of two and seven?

Multiples (3)

Worksheet Name: Date:

Write the multiples of four, up to 10 x 4:

Write the multiples of three, up to 10 x 3:

Write the multiples of eight, up to 10 x 8:

Write the multiples of nine, up to 10 x 9:

Write the multiples of six, up to 10 x 6:

Find the LCM (Lowest Common Multiple) of six and eight:

What is the LCM of four and nine?

What is the LCM of three and eight?

What is the LCM of six and nine?

What is the LCM of three and four?

Multiples (4)

Worksheet Name: Date:

Multiples of five always end in 5 or 0.

Multiples of ten always end in 0.

Multiples of twenty-five always end in 25,50,75 or 00.

Multiples of fifty always end in 50 or 00.

Multiples of a hundred always end in 00.

Look at this set of numbers.

13 75 280 185

68 500 1250 225

350 418 2000

950 1200 2475

Which of the numbers are multiples of ten?

Which of the numbers are multiples of five?

Which of the numbers are multiples of twenty-five?

Which of the numbers are multiples of fifty?

Which of the numbers are multiples of a hundred?

Square Numbers (1)

OHP Display

$1 \times 1 = 1$

Two sets of two can make a square shape.

We can say that two squared makes four.

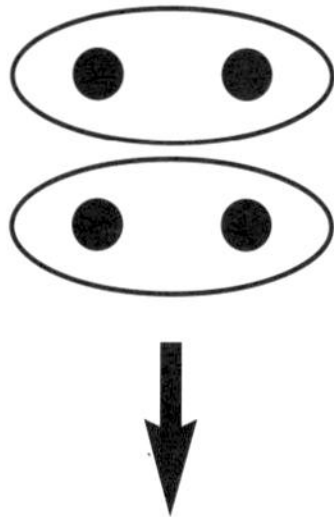

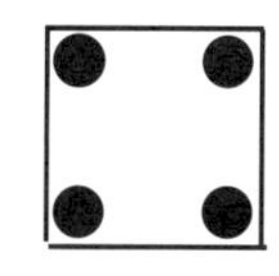

$2 \times 2 = 4$

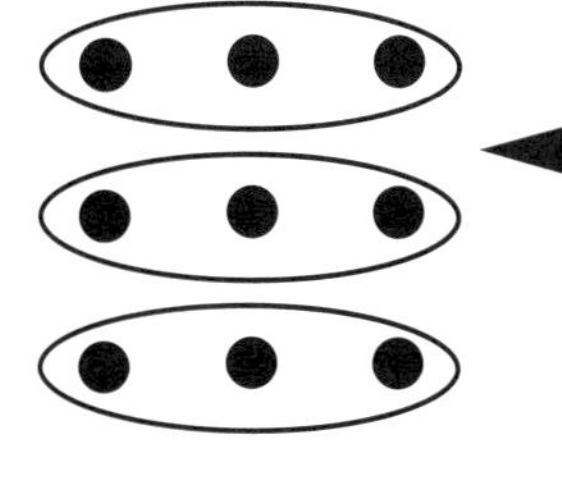

Three sets of three can make a square shape.

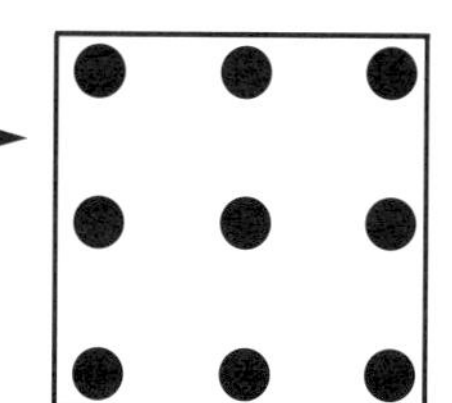

$3 \times 3 = 9$

Three squared makes nine.

This is the symbol for 'squared'.

$3^2 = 9$

Square Numbers (2)

Worksheet Name: Date:

$4 \times 4 = 16$

Four squared makes sixteen.

$4^2 = 16$

Complete these square number questions:

$5^2 = 5 \times 5 =$ 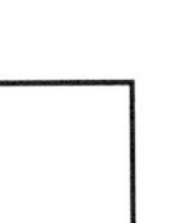

$6^2 =$ ☐ x ☐ = 

$7^2 =$ ☐ x ☐ = 

$8^2 =$ ☐ x ☐ = ☐

$9^2 =$ ☐ x ☐ = ☐

$10^2 =$ ☐ x ☐ = ☐

$11^2 =$ ☐ x ☐ = ☐

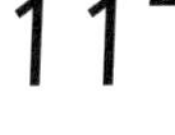
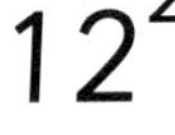
$12^2 =$ ☐ x ☐ = ☐

$0^2 =$ ☐ x ☐ = ☐

$1^2 =$ ☐ x ☐ = ☐

$2^2 =$ ☐ x 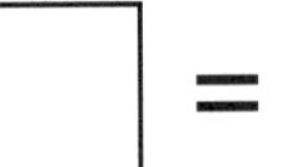 = ☐

$3^2 =$ 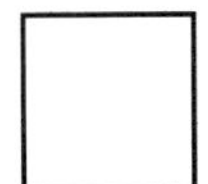 x 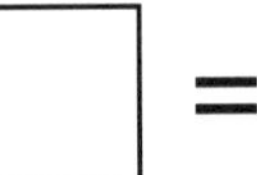 = ☐

Square Numbers (3)

Worksheet Name: Date:

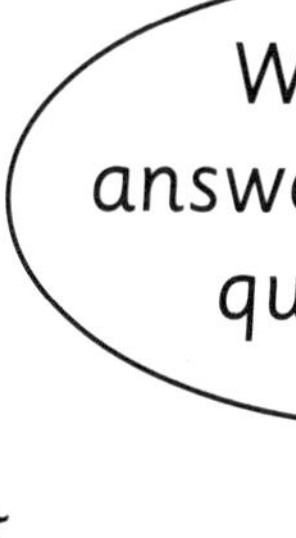

Write the answers to these questions.

ⓐ $2^2 =$ ☐ ⓑ $8^2 =$ ☐

ⓒ $4^2 =$ ☐ ⓓ $7^2 =$ ☐

ⓔ $10^2 =$ ☐ ⓕ $6^2 =$ ☐

ⓖ $5^2 =$ ☐ ⓗ $3^2 =$ ☐

ⓘ $1^2 =$ ☐ ⓙ $12^2 =$ ☐

ⓚ $9^2 =$ ☐ ⓛ $11^2 =$ ☐

ⓜ $4^2 + 2^2 =$ ☐

ⓝ $6^2 + 5^2 =$ ☐

ⓞ $3^2 + 4^2 =$ ☐

ⓟ $12^2 + 1^2 =$ ☐

ⓠ $9^2 + 11^2 =$ ☐

ⓡ $7^2 - 6^2 =$ ☐

ⓢ $12^2 - 8^2 =$ ☐

ⓣ $10^2 - 6^2 =$ ☐

ⓤ $9^2 - 4^2 =$ ☐

ⓥ Two of the answers are square numbers themselves. Which ones?

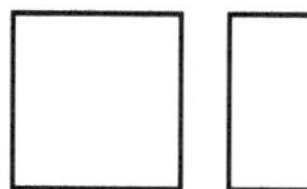

Square Roots

Extension Worksheet

Name: Date:

The square of five is twenty-five: $5^2 = 25$

The square root of twenty-five is five: $\sqrt{25} = 5$

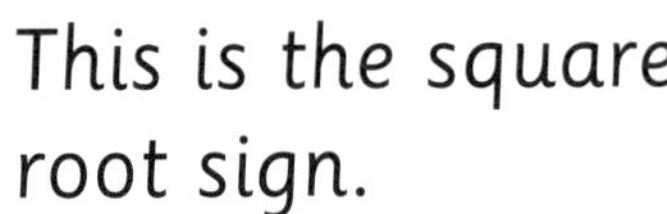

This is the square root sign.

Answer these questions:

(a) $\sqrt{49} =$ ☐ (b) $\sqrt{100} =$ ☐ (c) $\sqrt{64} =$ ☐ (d) $\sqrt{36} =$ ☐

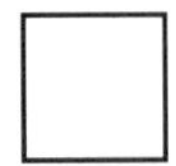

(e) $\sqrt{121} =$ ☐ (f) $\sqrt{9} =$ ☐ (g) $\sqrt{4} =$ ☐ (h) $\sqrt{144} =$ ☐

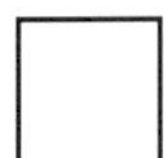

(i) $\sqrt{81} =$ ☐ (j) $\sqrt{16} =$ ☐ (k) $\sqrt{1} =$ ☐ (l) $\sqrt{625} =$ ☐

Factors (1)

OHP Display

16

1	X	16
16	X	1
2	X	8
8	X	2
4	X	4

The factors of 16 are:

1, 2, 4, 8, 16

Factors (2)

Worksheet Name: Date:

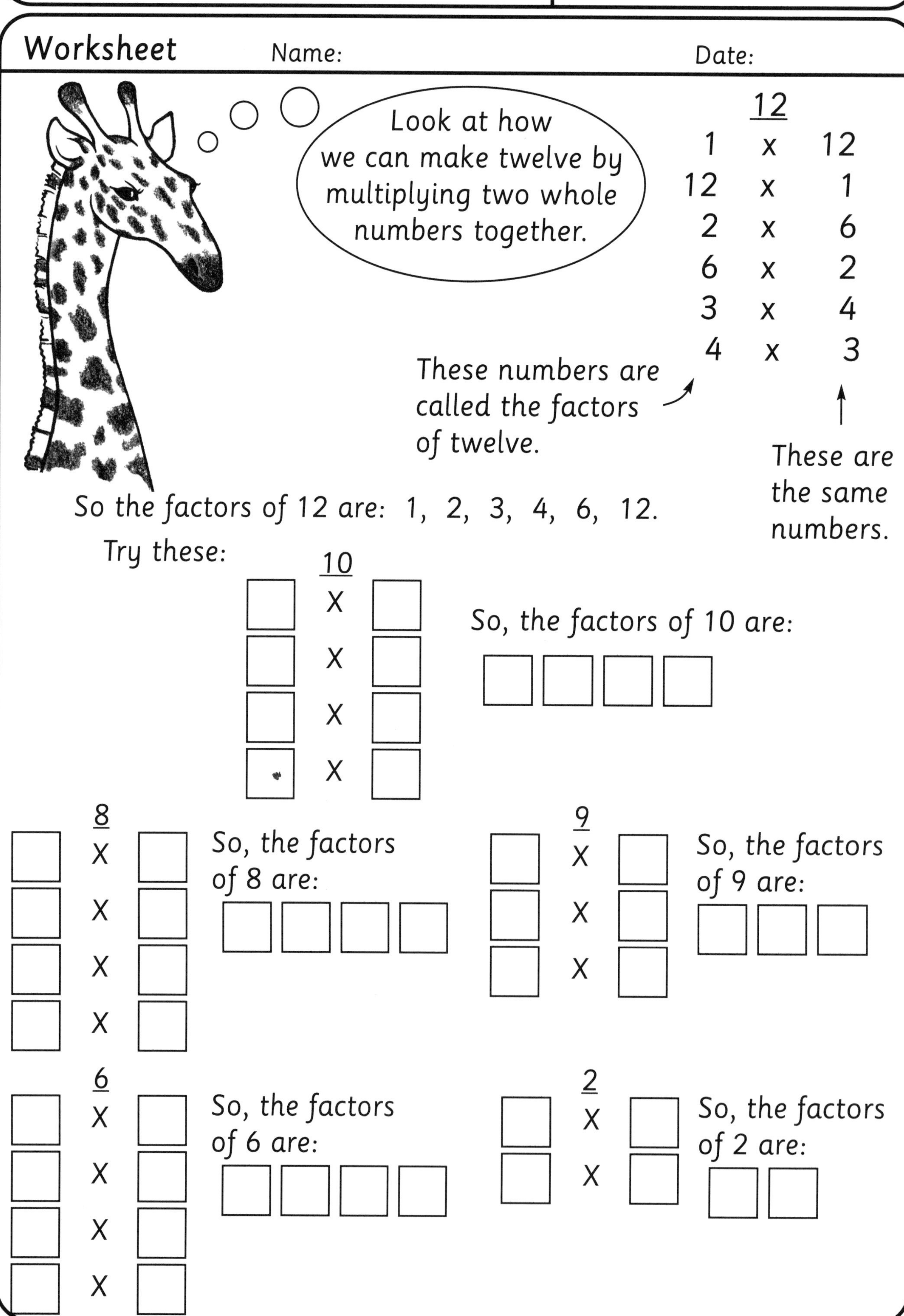

  www.acblack.com

Factors (3)

Worksheet
Name:
Date:
Find the factors of 36.
36
So the factors of 36 are:
144
Find the factors of 144.
So the factors of 144 are:

Factors and Prime Numbers (1)

OHP Display

There's something special about all these numbers.

Look at the factors of each number:

11

☐ X ☐

☐ X ☐

The factors of 11 are:

☐ and ☐

7

☐ X ☐

☐ X ☐

The factors of 7 are:

☐ and ☐

2

☐ X ☐

☐ X ☐

The factors of 2 are:

☐ and ☐

17

☐ X ☐

☐ X ☐

The factors of 17 are:

☐ and ☐

Each of these numbers has only two factors: itself and one.

Numbers like these are called prime numbers.

Factors and Prime Numbers (2)

Worksheet Name: Date:

Look at how we can make the number 14 by multiplying together two whole numbers.

7 x 2 1 x 14

14

2 x 7 14 x 1

These are the numbers we have used: 1, 2, 7, 14.
These numbers are called the factors of 14.

List the factors of each of the numbers below:

10 □ □ □ □

8 □ □ □ □

4 □ □ □

3 □ □

16 □ □ □ □ □

7 □ □

24 □ □ □ □ □ □ □ □

19 □ □

Number 7 has only two factors, itself and 1.

Because of this it is called a prime number.

Which of the other numbers above are prime numbers?

□ and □

Prime Numbers

Worksheet Name: Date:

Prime numbers are special because they have exactly two factors, themselves and 1. 1 is not a prime because it only has one factor.
Prime numbers are unusual in that they do not make a pattern.

A Greek astronomer named **Eratostenes**, who lived 2100 years ago, devised the following method for finding prime numbers. It is called **the sieve of Eratostenes.**

Using the grid below:

(i) **Cross out** the number 1 as it is not prime

(ii) Leave 2 as it is a prime number but **cross out every multiple of 2** (4,6,8..)

(iii) Leave 3 as it is a prime number but **cross out every multiple of 3** (6,9,12..)

(iv) Leave 5 as it is a prime number but **cross out every multiple of 5** (10,15..)

(v) Leave 7 as it is a prime number but **cross out every multiple of 7** (14,21..)

1	2	3	4	5	6	7	8	9	10
11	12	13	14	15	16	17	18	19	20
21	22	23	24	25	26	27	28	29	30
31	32	33	34	35	36	37	38	39	40
41	42	43	44	45	46	47	48	49	50
51	52	53	54	55	56	57	58	59	60
61	62	63	64	65	66	67	68	69	70
71	72	73	74	75	76	77	78	79	80
81	82	83	84	85	86	87	88	89	90
91	92	93	94	95	96	97	98	99	100

The numbers which are left uncrossed are all prime numbers.

List all the prime numbers between 1 and 100:

What is the only **even** prime number?

Multiplication Speed Tests

Worksheet Name: Date:

Time yourself on each day's test.

See if you can improve by the end of the week.

Monday	Tuesday	Wednesday	Thursday	Friday
2 x 4 =	3 x 2 =	8 x 8 =	11 x 4 =	3 x 6 =
3 x 9 =	8 x 9 =	3 x 4 =	2 x 8 =	4 x 8 =
7 x 8 =	7 x 6 =	7 x 9 =	3 x 9 =	7 x 3 =
9 x 4 =	4 x 3 =	10 x 7 =	5 x 7 =	12 x 3 =
10 x 7 =	9 x 8 =	12 x 12 =	8 x 6 =	9 x 4 =
6 x 9 =	11 x 11 =	3 x 7 =	5 x 5 =	8 x 7 =
8 x 8 =	6 x 4 =	6 x 8 =	6 x 9 =	6 x 9 =
5 x 4 =	9 x 4 =	5 x 9 =	12 x 7 =	11 x 10 =
8 x 6 =	8 x 7 =	4 x 9 =	5 x 8 =	3 x 8 =
7 x 3 =	6 x 6 =	7 x 8 =	7 x 3 =	9 x 5 =
9 x 2 =	3 x 9 =	8 x 4 =	6 x 5 =	7 x 2 =
12 x 4 =	9 x 6 =	9 x 6 =	8 x 4 =	6 x 3 =
9 x 9 =	5 x 5 =	7 x 3 =	7 x 7 =	5 x 8 =
7 x 5 =	7 x 4 =	9 x 9 =	3 x 8 =	6 x 7 =
6 x 6 =	9 x 5 =	5 x 7 =	9 x 2 =	8 x 4 =
8 x 5 =	8 x 4 =	6 x 5 =	8 x 9 =	3 x 5 =
3 x 9 =	10 x 9 =	8 x 7 =	10 x 12 =	8 x 6 =
9 x 6 =	4 x 4 =	2 x 4 =	3 x 5 =	8 x 9 =
8 x 2 =	8 x 6 =	3 x 9 =	6 x 7 =	4 x 4 =
7 x 4 =	7 x 7 =	8 x 9 =	5 x 8 =	5 x 7 =
Time taken:	Time taken:	Time taken:	Time taken:	Time taken:

Division Speed Tests

Worksheet Name: Date:

Time yourself on each day's test.

See if you can improve by the end of the week.

Monday	Tuesday	Wednesday	Thursday	Friday
72 ÷ 8 =	21 ÷ 3 =	28 ÷ 7 =	30 ÷ 6 =	54 ÷ 9 =
40 ÷ 12 =	144 ÷ 12 =	18 ÷ 3 =	72 ÷ 9 =	81 ÷ 9 =
63 ÷ 9 =	36 ÷ 9 =	32 ÷ 4 =	25 ÷ 5 =	64 ÷ 8 =
24 ÷ 6 =	25 ÷ 5 =	48 ÷ 6 =	48 ÷ 8 =	42 ÷ 6 =
110 ÷ 10 =	72 ÷ 9 =	72 ÷ 9 =	8 ÷ 2 =	16 ÷ 4 =
45 ÷ 9 =	96 ÷ 8 =	45 ÷ 9 =	24 ÷ 4 =	21 ÷ 3 =
28 ÷ 7 =	63 ÷ 7 =	24 ÷ 6 =	36 ÷ 6 =	45 ÷ 5 =
36 ÷ 4 =	28 ÷ 7 =	35 ÷ 5 =	56 ÷ 7 =	144 ÷ 12 =
56 ÷ 8 =	48 ÷ 6 =	64 ÷ 8 =	33 ÷ 3 =	72 ÷ 9 =
77 ÷ 7 =	16 ÷ 4 =	132 ÷ 12 =	84 ÷ 7 =	28 ÷ 7 =
48 ÷ 6 =	56 ÷ 7 =	84 ÷ 12 =	32 ÷ 8 =	18 ÷ 3 =
54 ÷ 9 =	64 ÷ 8 =	56 ÷ 7 =	54 ÷ 6 =	6 ÷ 2 =
18 ÷ 3 =	27 ÷ 9 =	36 ÷ 9 =	108 ÷ 12 =	72 ÷ 6 =
18 ÷ 2 =	8 ÷ 4 =	21 ÷ 7 =	42 ÷ 6 =	48 ÷ 6 =
32 ÷ 8 =	36 ÷ 6 =	14 ÷ 2 =	40 ÷ 8 =	120 ÷ 10 =
56 ÷ 8 =	42 ÷ 7 =	54 ÷ 9 =	121 ÷ 11 =	35 ÷ 5 =
81 ÷ 9 =	63 ÷ 9 =	40 ÷ 8 =	24 ÷ 3 =	48 ÷ 4 =
28 ÷ 4 =	72 ÷ 8 =	42 ÷ 6 =	35 ÷ 5 =	56 ÷ 7 =
12 ÷ 2 =	35 ÷ 5 =	55 ÷ 11 =	21 ÷ 7 =	24 ÷ 6 =
21 ÷ 3 =	81 ÷ 9 =	27 ÷ 3 =	63 ÷ 7 =	32 ÷ 8 =
Time taken:	Time taken:	Time taken:	Time taken:	Time taken:

